I padded Los Angeles

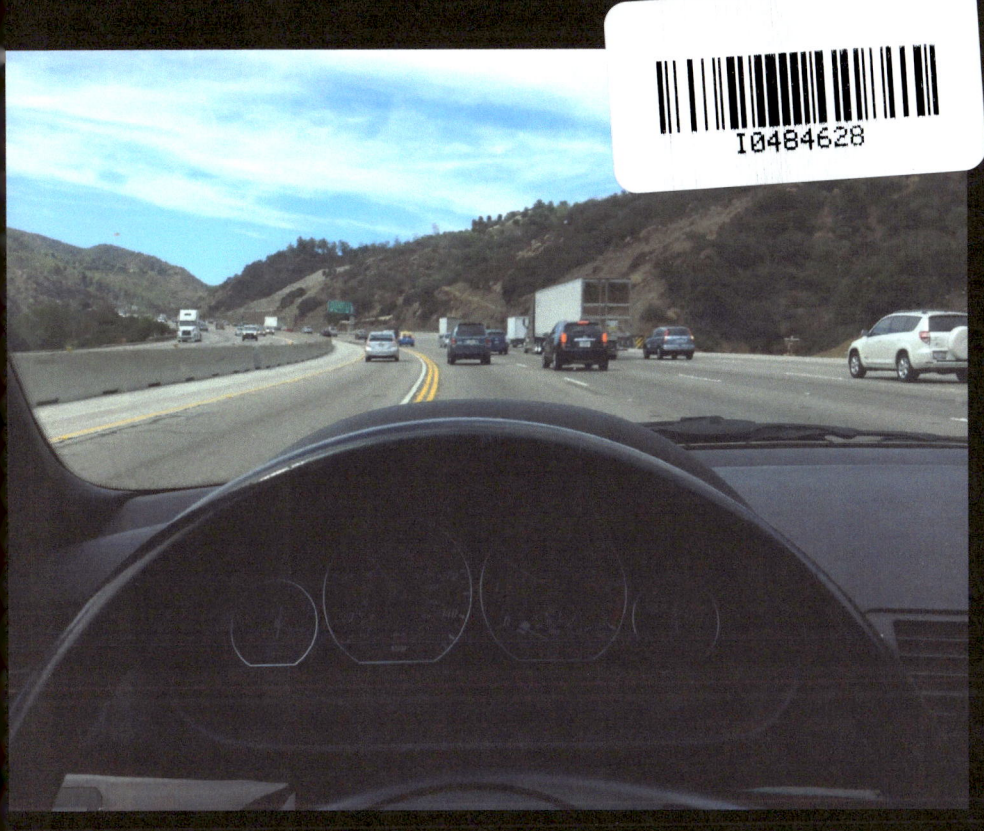

Every day sights in LA

By Michael Carey

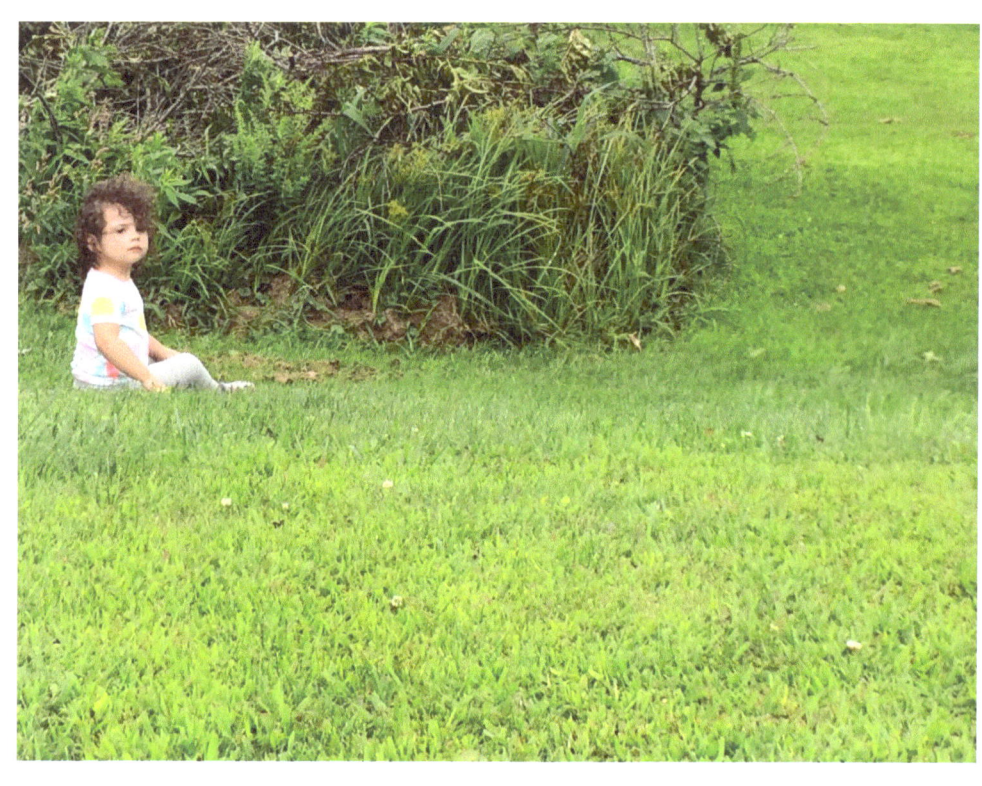

This book is dedicated to

my wonderful wife Chava

and our beautiful little girl

Claire and her big sister Taylor.

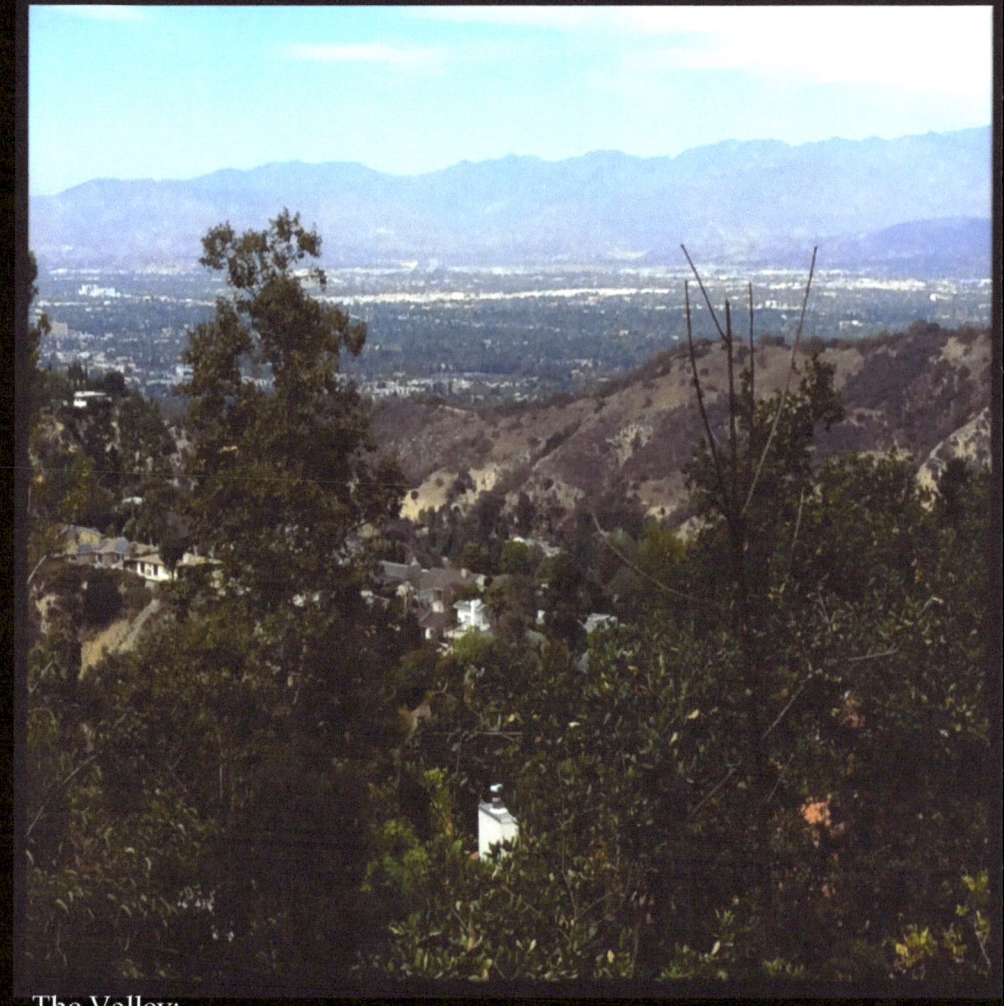

The Valley:

This is a shot from the 405 freeway of the San Fernando Valley. Famous in the 1980's for the birth of the valley girl .

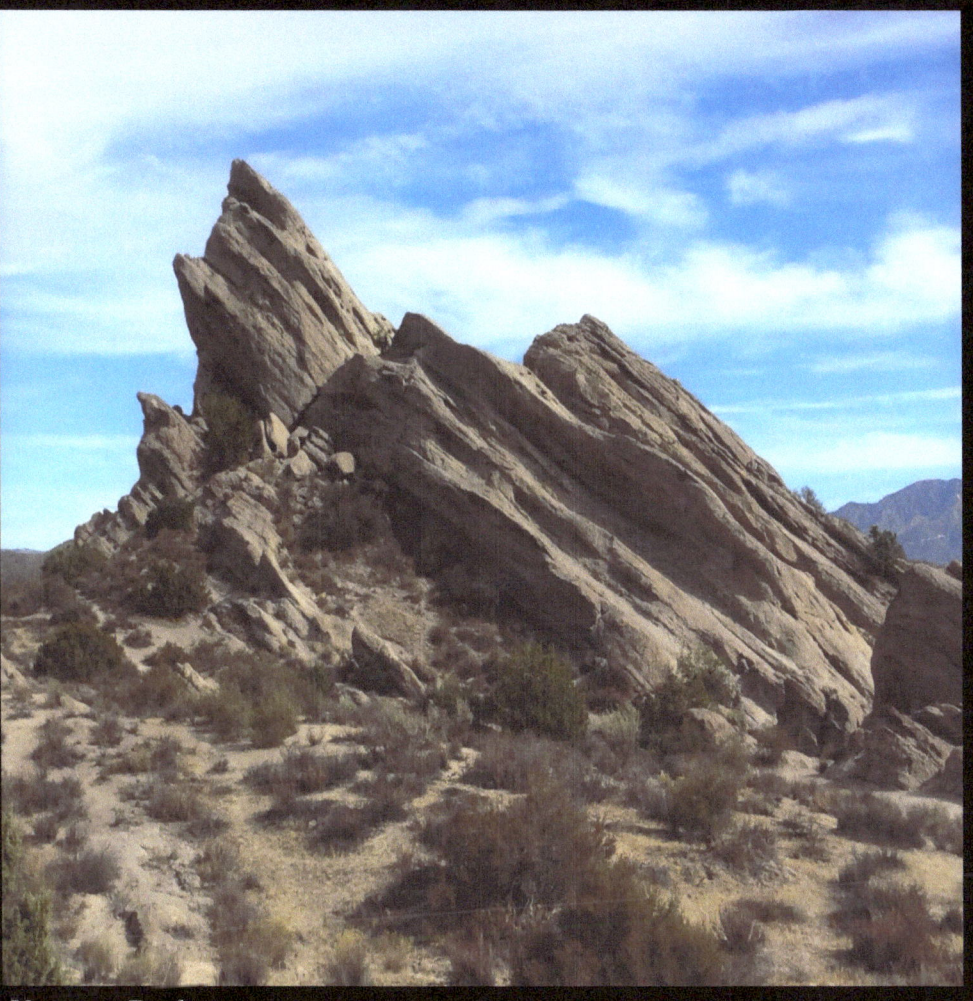

Vasquez Rocks:

Just about every Sci fi movie, tv show and western has used this historic
site as a background for production. You can see this rock formation
from the 14 freeway and access it from the town of Agua Dulce. The last
big movie to be shot here was Star Trek by J. J. Abrams .

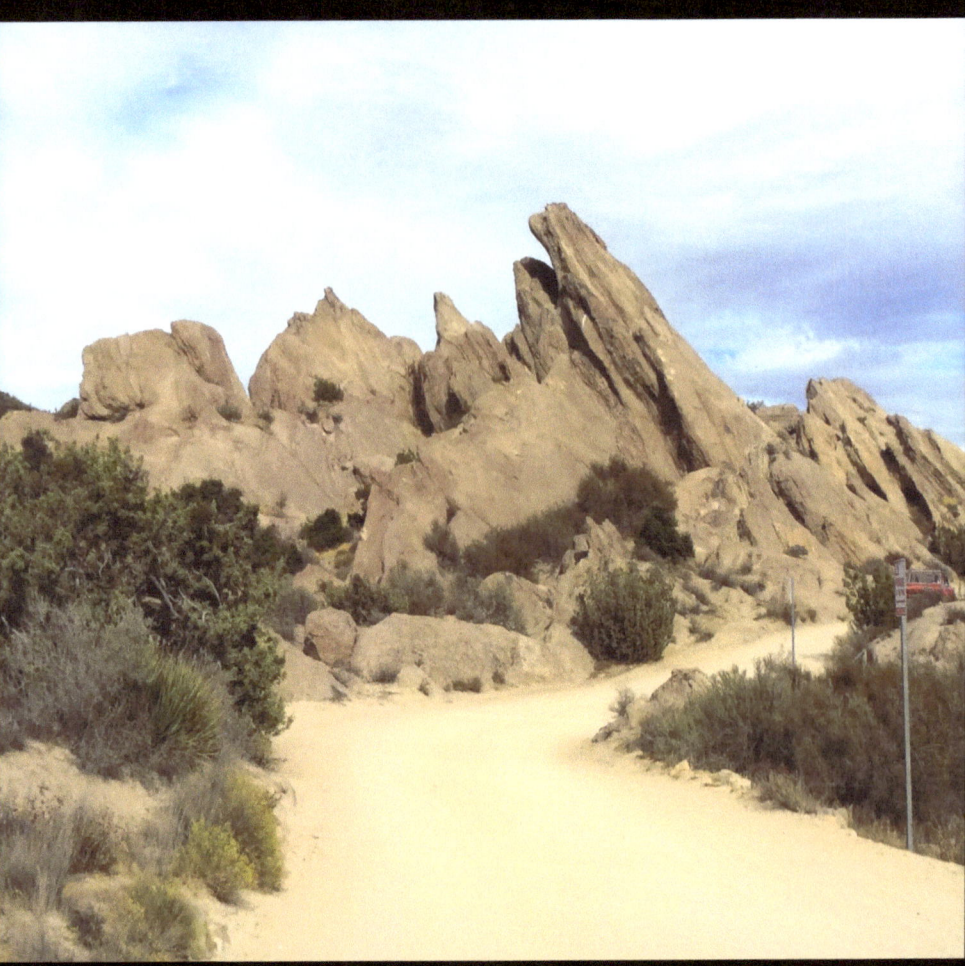

Another shot to give you a sense of scale. It really does look alien.

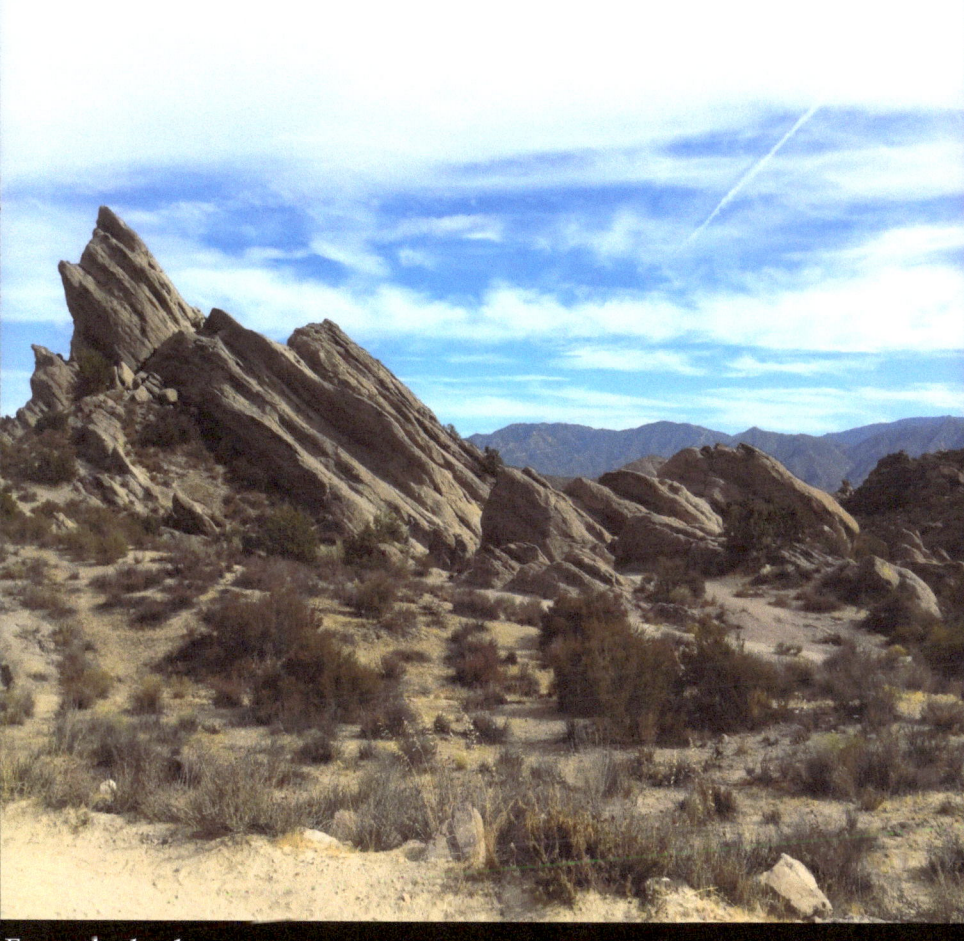

From the back.

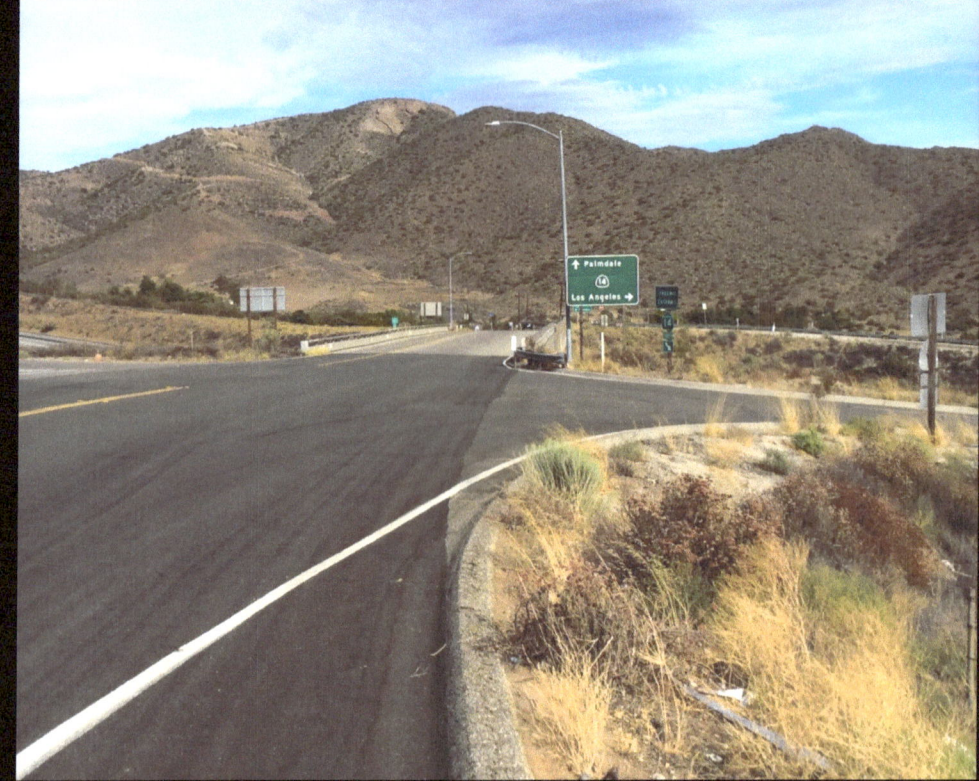

On Ramp:

California is full of these, this on happens to be the on ramp leading to the 14 freeway form Agua Dulce. The freeway system in California is so vast that there seems to be a infinite number of ways to reach anywhere you would like to go. There's even a system called the four level that looks like a bunch of freeways stacked on top of each other.

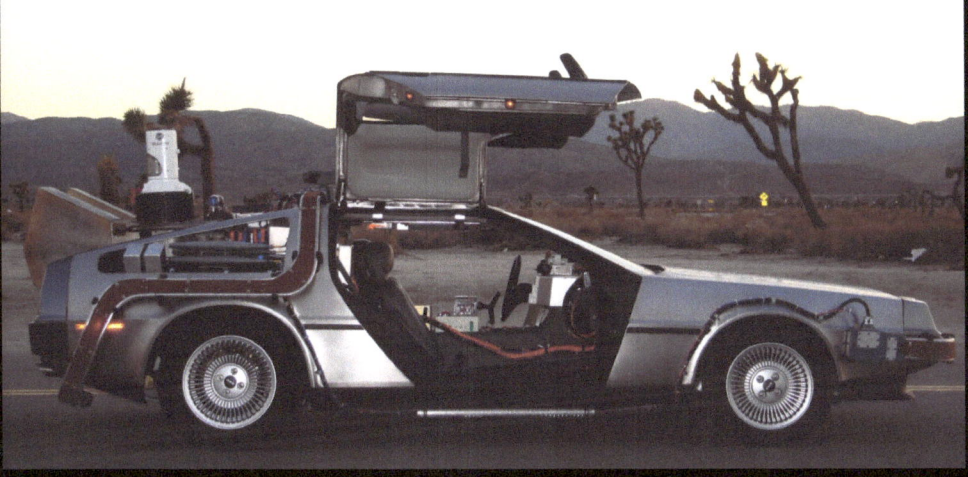

Classic cars of California:

One thing about California that sets it apart from the rest of the world is it's classic car culture. Summers are filled with the endless car shows and cruse nights that only this state can host the way it does. This car, a classic in the 80's and shown here as the car from Back to the Future is a fine example of California's love of cars in film as hot rods and fine re-stored classics.

The sunset at El Segundo beach.

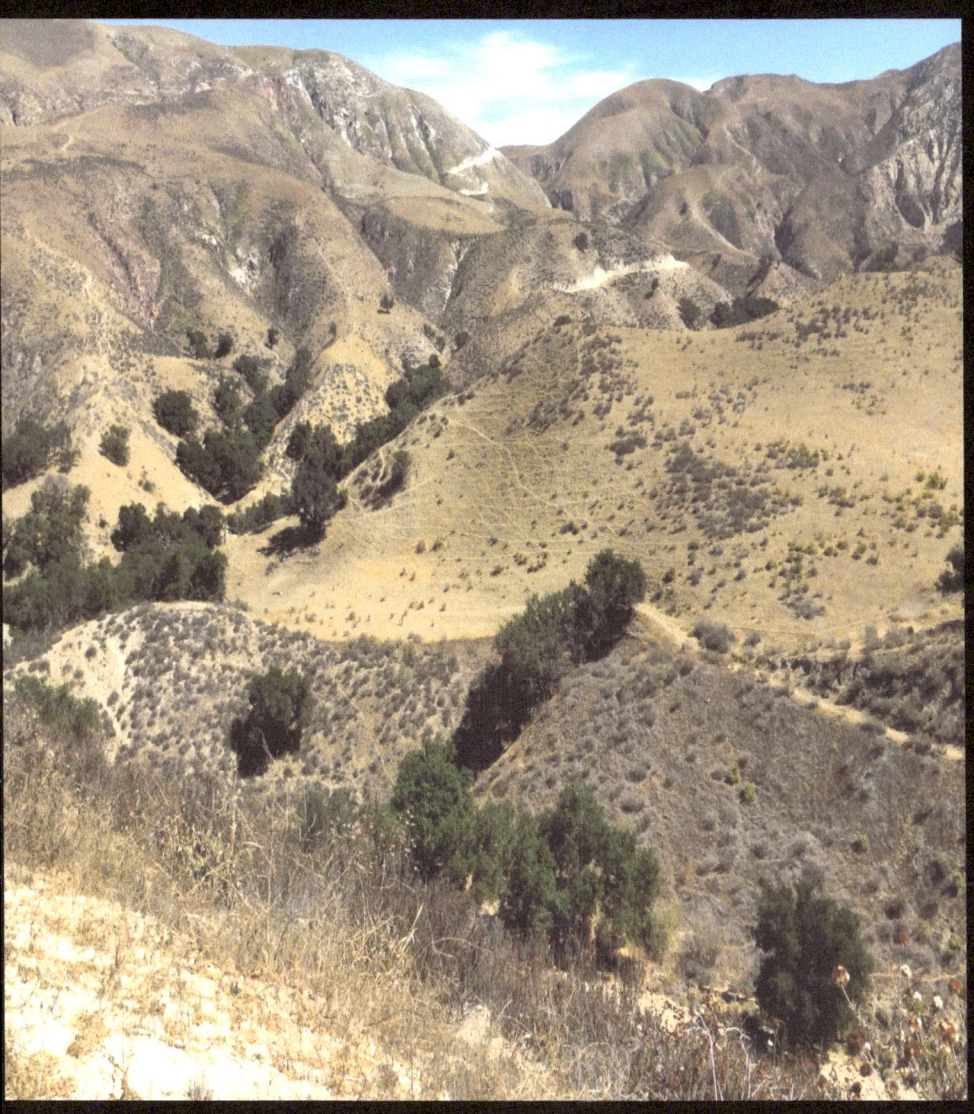

The canyons outside of Fillmore. Although brown from drought these landscapes are still impressive stretches of land.

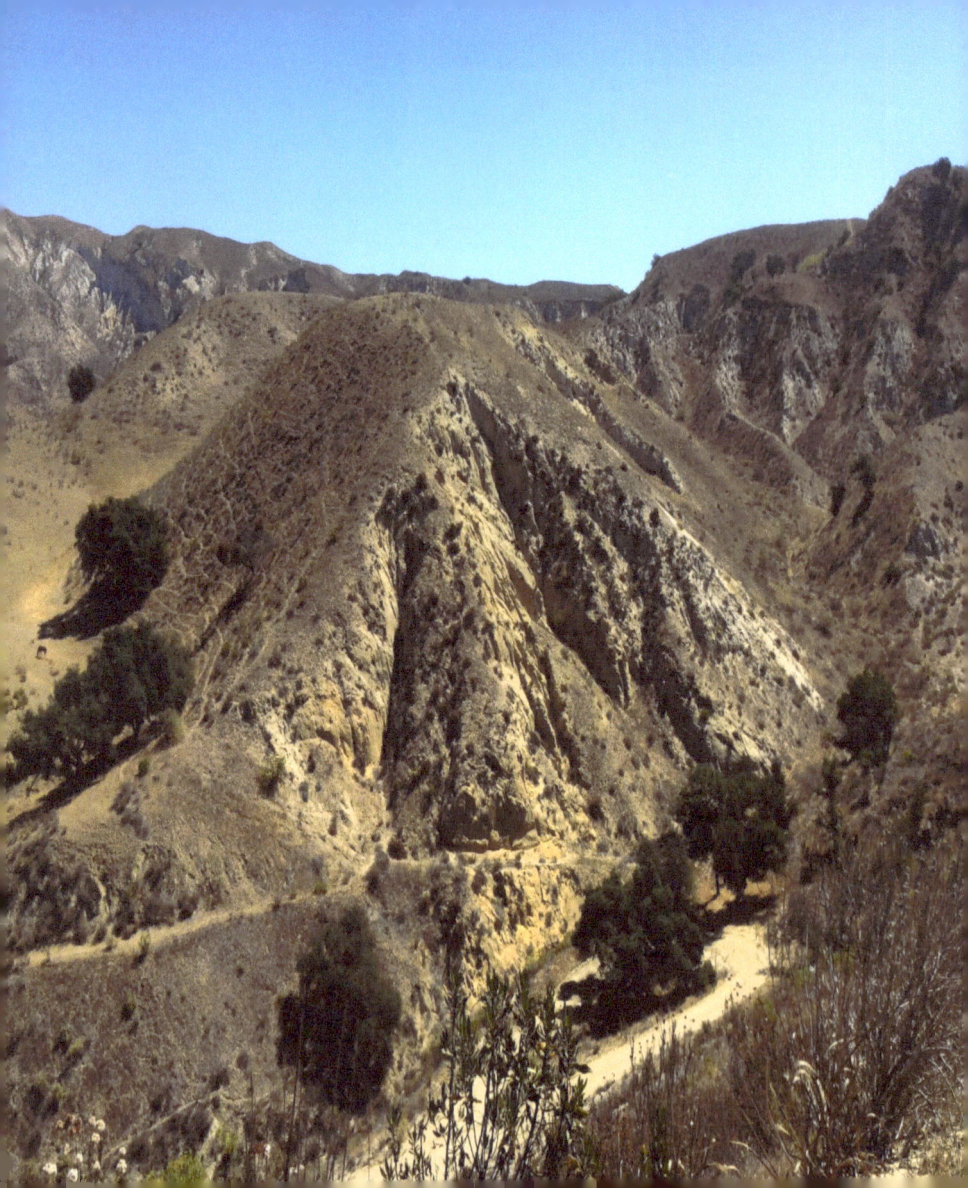

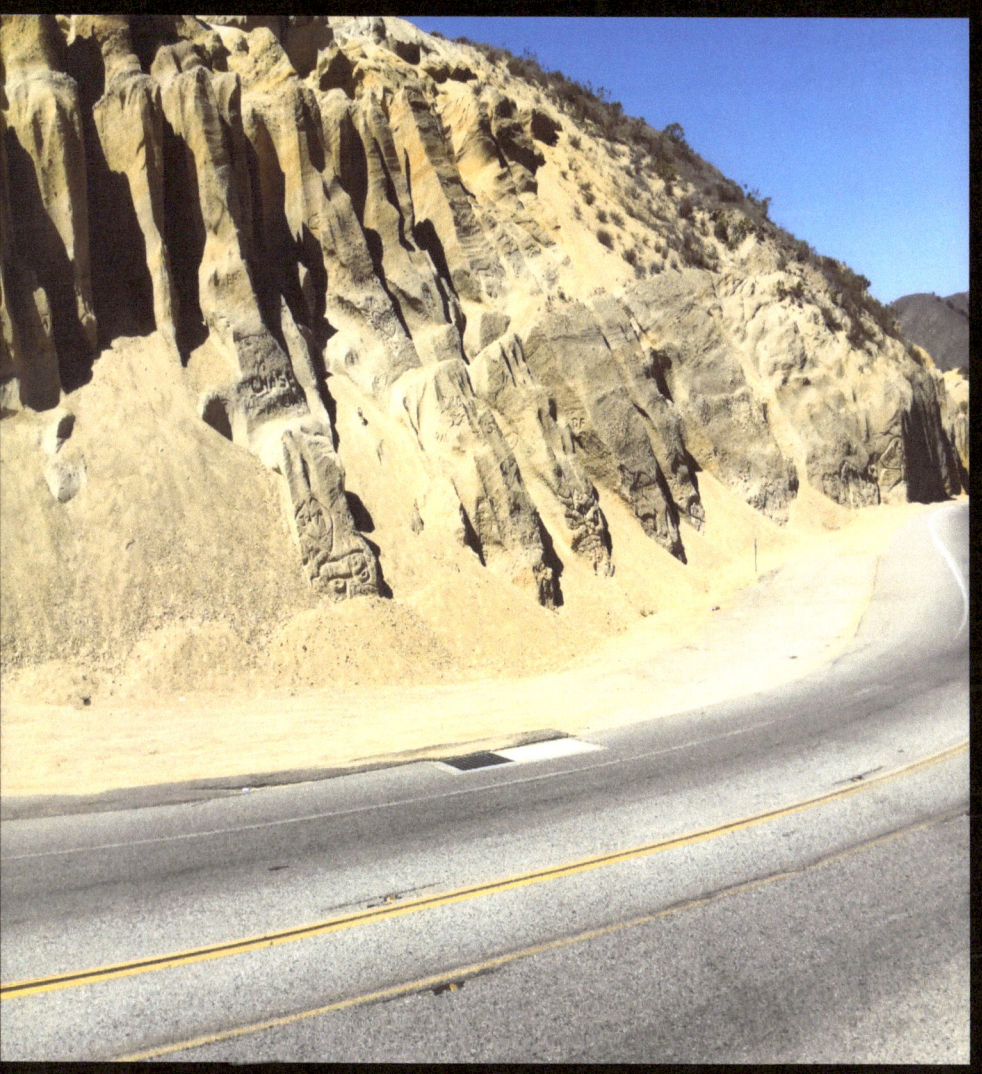

The sand stone and art work of grimes canyon.

The following pictures are of the sandstone art carvings of grimes canyon. Some of these are nothing more than graffiti and people pouring out their undying love for another and some are beautiful 3D art from some very creative people. I Imagine some of these artists have some really great pumpkins on Halloween.

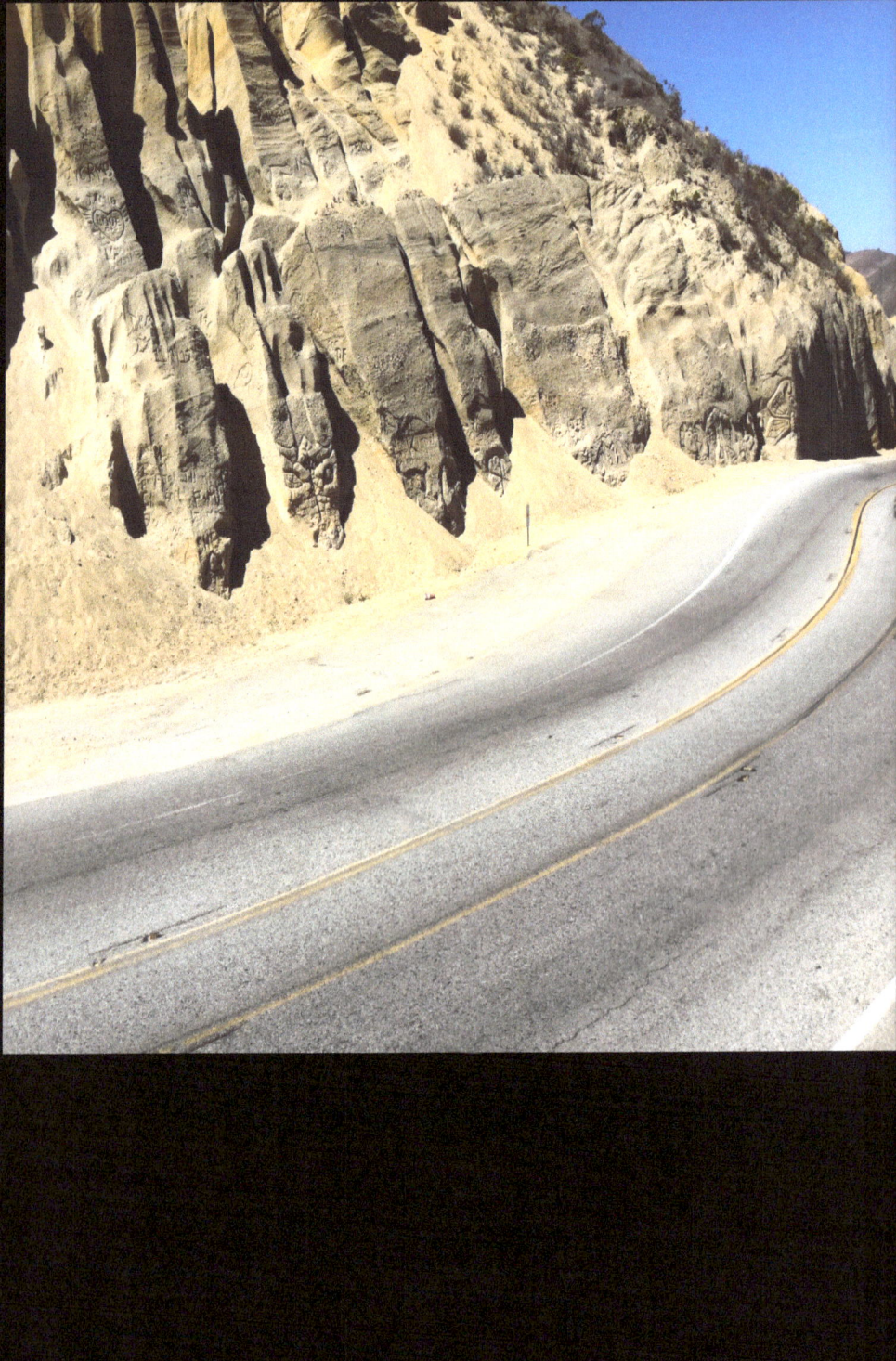

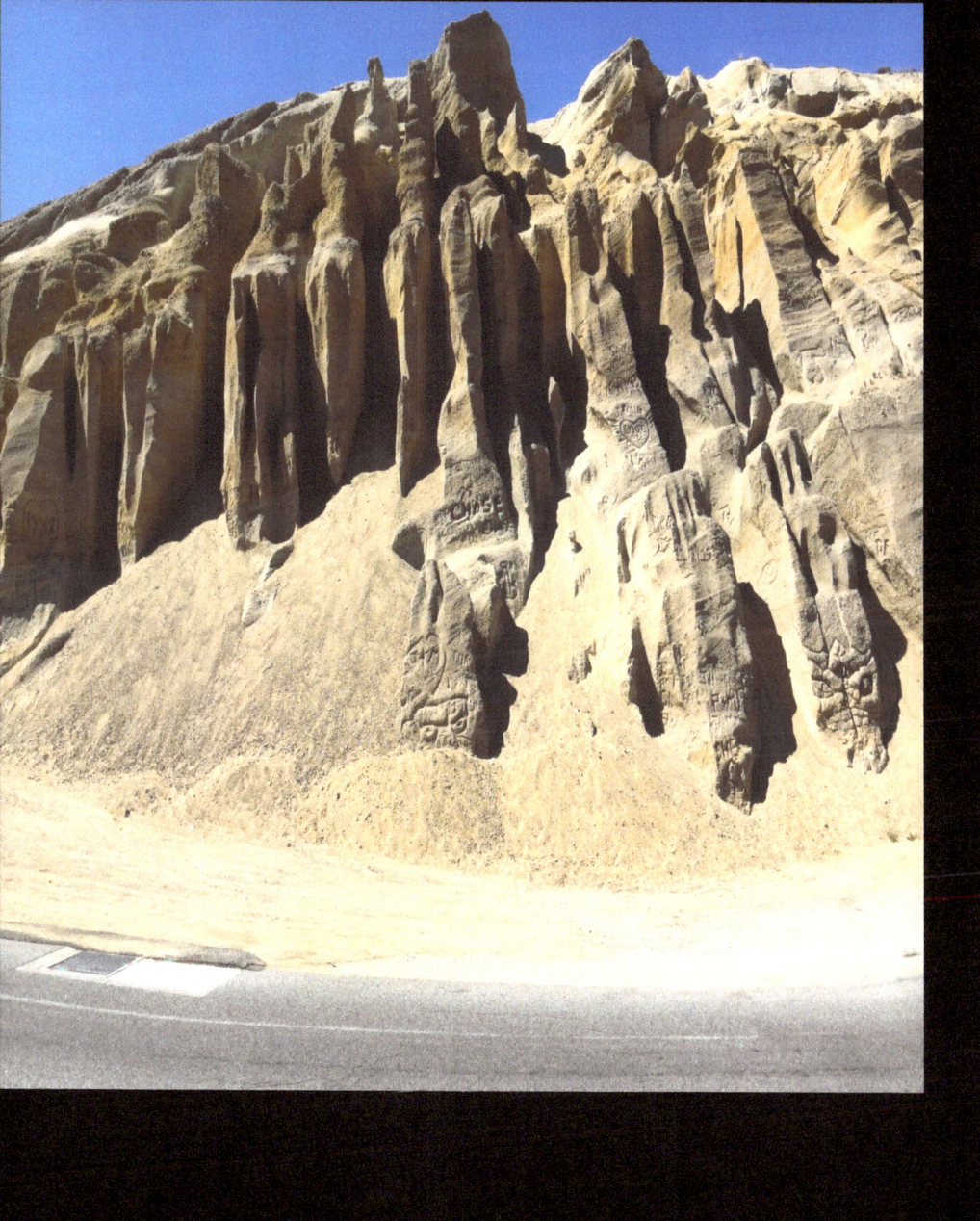

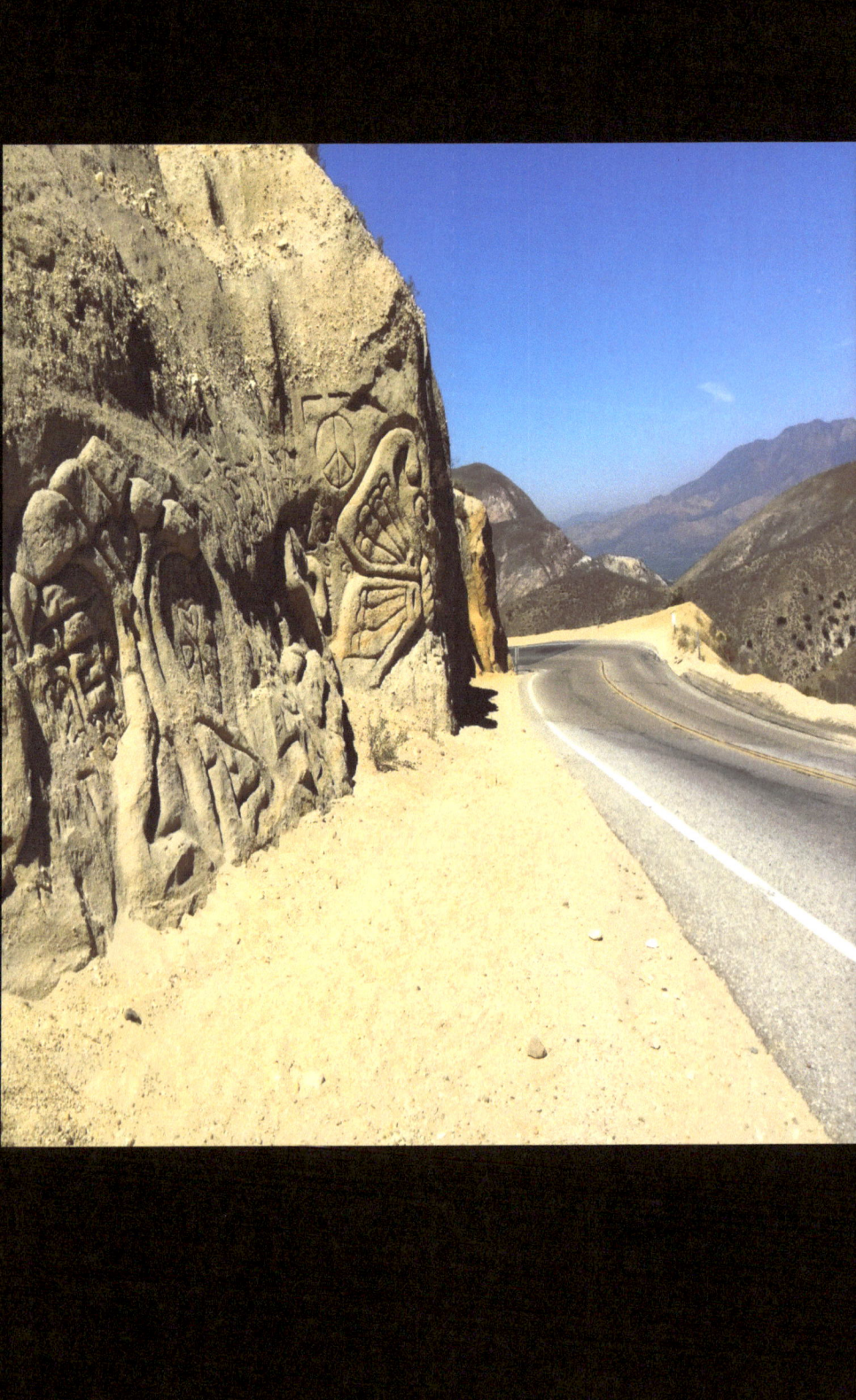

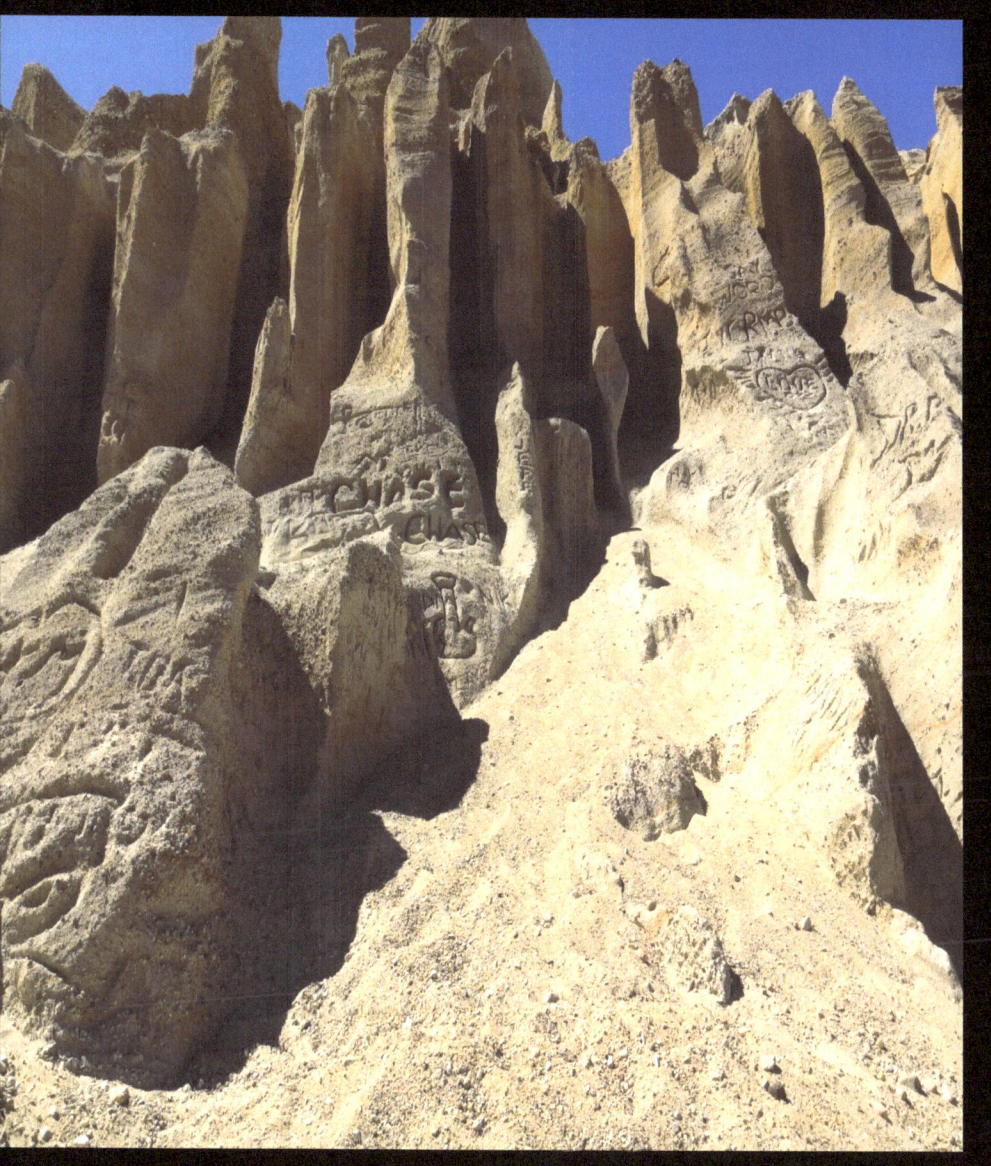

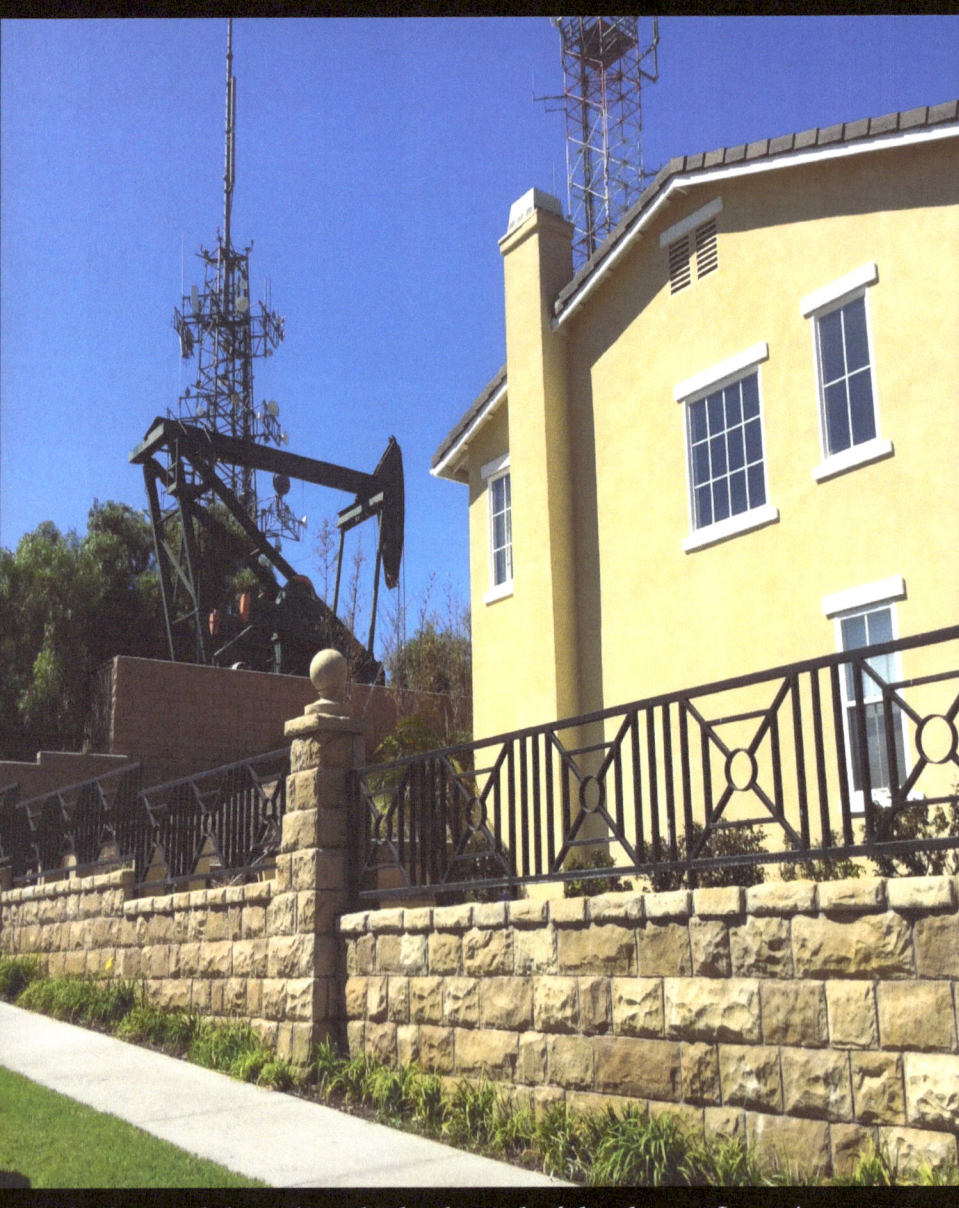

Yes that's an oil derrick in the back yard of that home. In various areas around California oil is still very much being pumped out of the ground. This shot was taken in Signal hill , but its a sight you'll find here and there and quite often in the city of Long Beach.

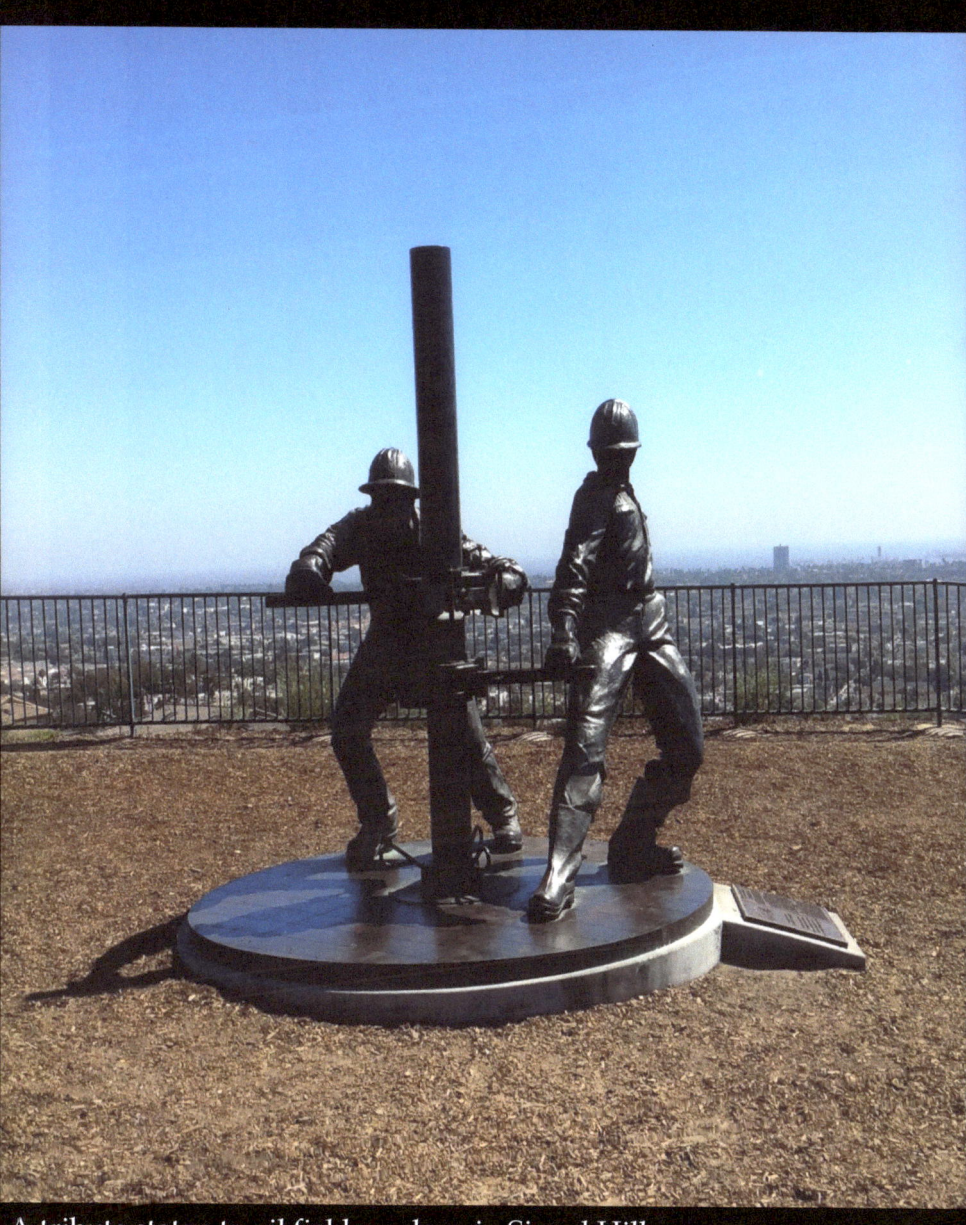

A tribute statue to oil field workers in Signal Hill

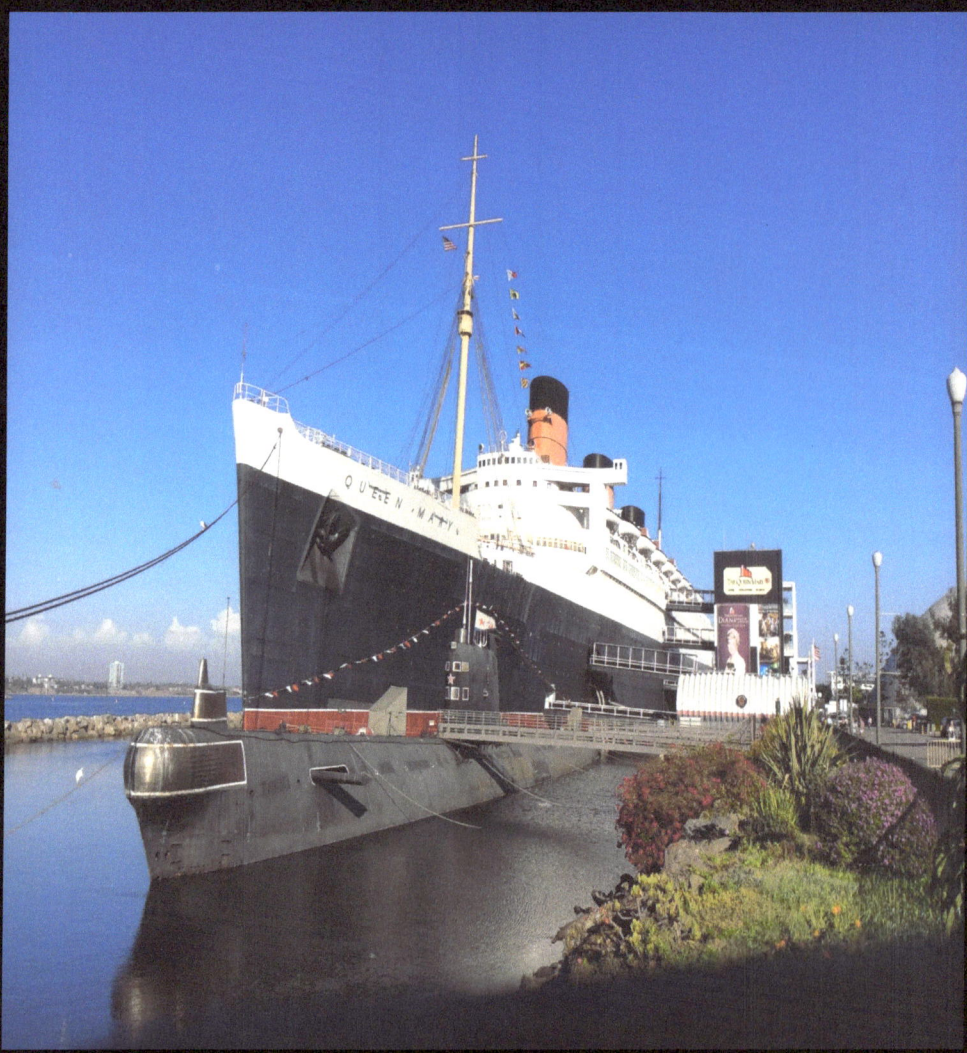

The Queen Mary:

On display in Long Beach along with a Russian Submarine. Both of these have been long time exhibits in the area. Before the Submarine arrived there was the famed spruce goose. The invention from aircraft designer Howard Hughes. The queen Mary is a functioning hotel that offers much for those looking for an event venue.

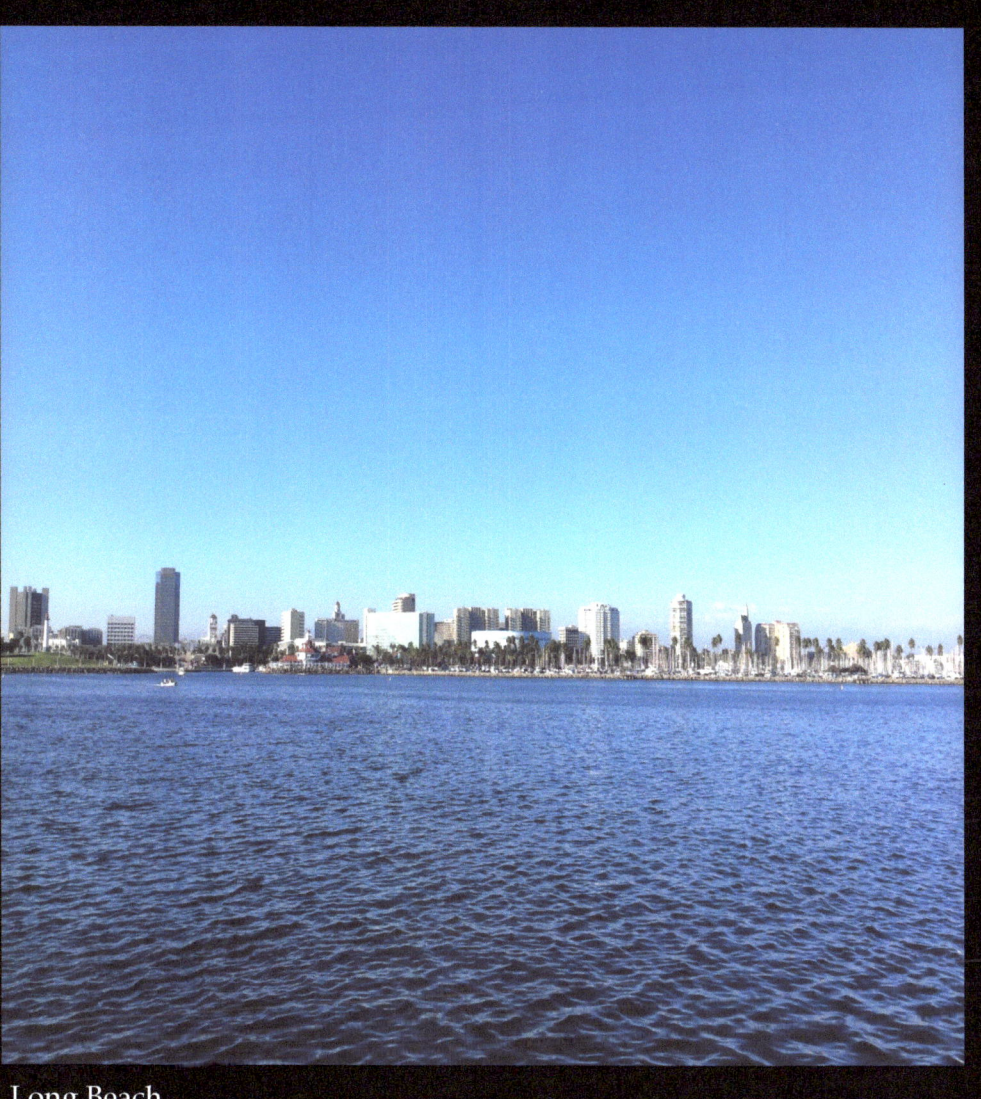

Long Beach

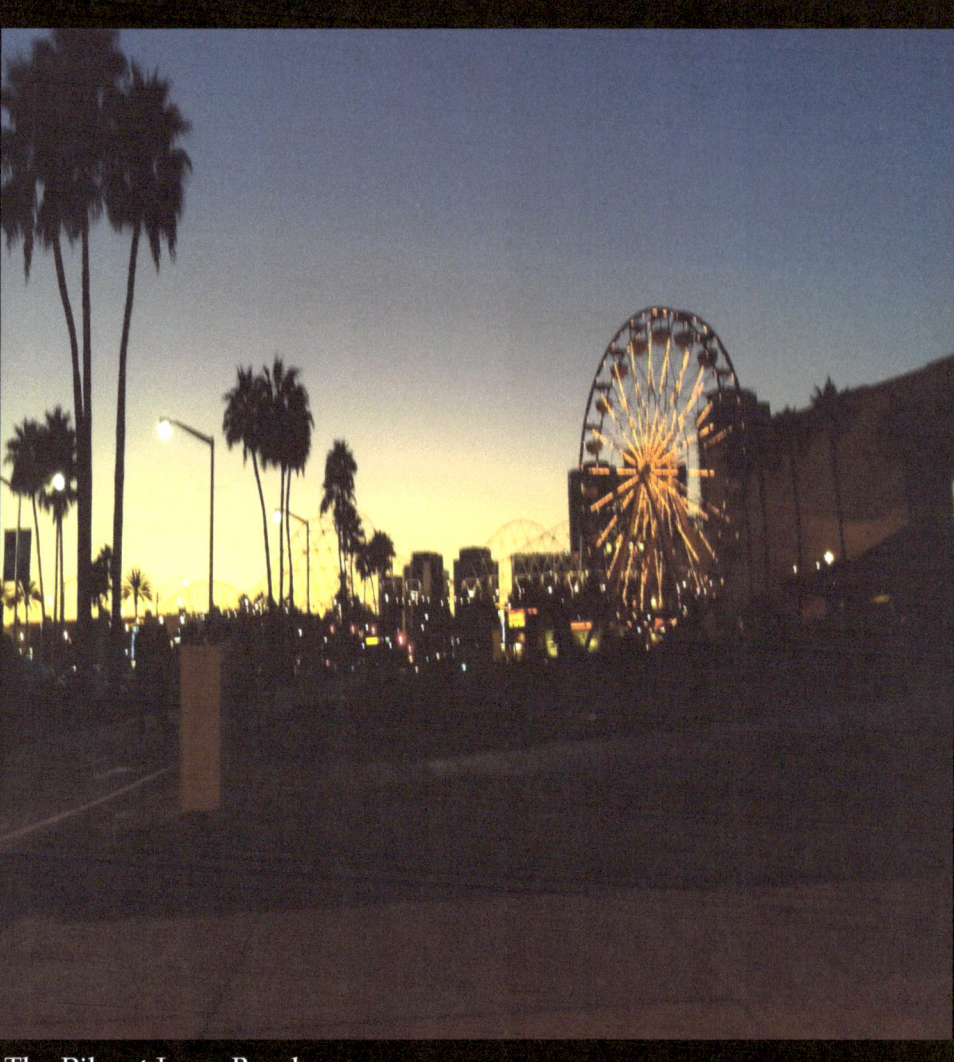

The Pike at Long Beach :

On this site in the 1960's was the site of a public pool that was filled with ocean water called the plunge. It was a favorite place for the community to get some leisure time in.

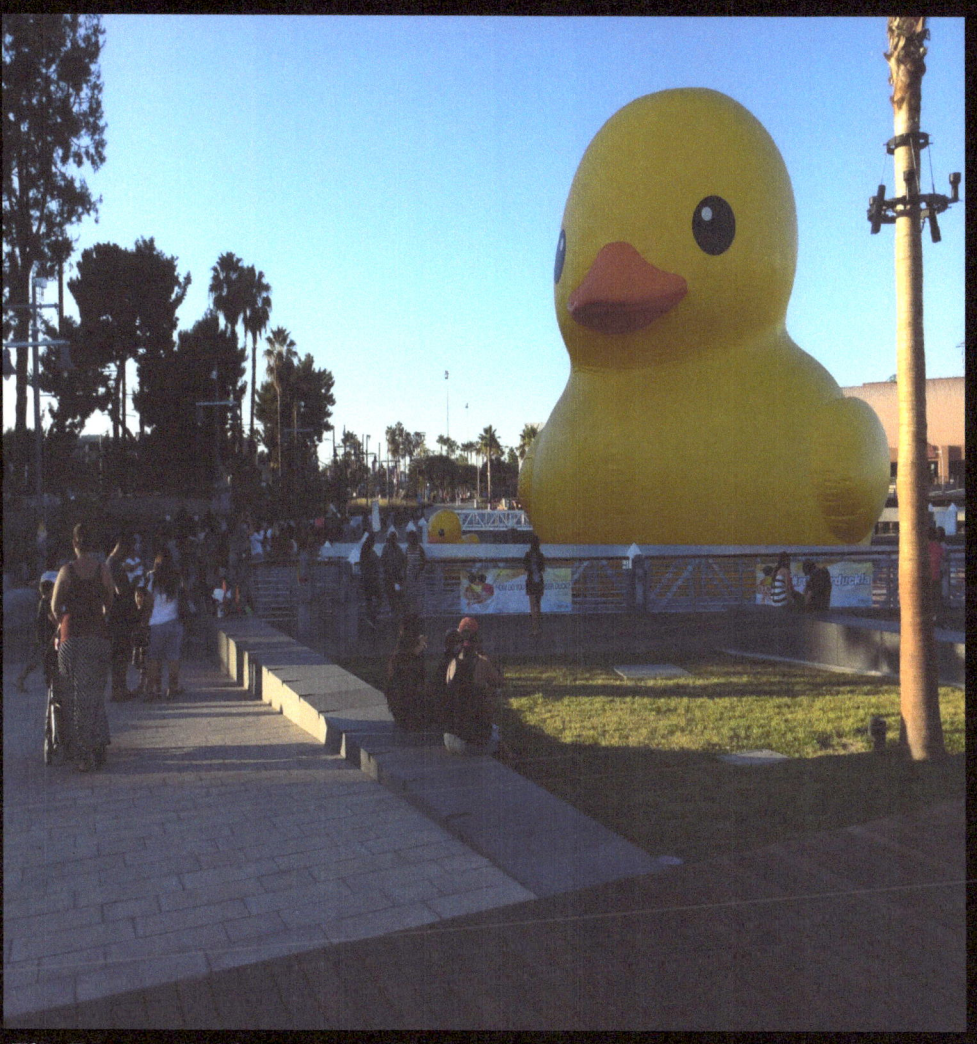

The Famous Duck:

This is the inflatable rubber duck making its way all-around the world.
Here it is docked in Long Beach.

Many Thanks to:

My wife for believing in me, my daughters for all of their special smiles,

My family for all the support in all of my

Many endeavors, no matter how crazy they may seem, and

All of the many friends I'm so lucky to have. I couldn't do half of the

Things I do without your encouragement

And help. You guys are all great!!